# Poems to Compare and Contrast

## selected by Brian Moses

## Contents

LONGMAN

KV-193-187

# For Dilberta

*Biggest of the Elephants at London Zoo*

The walking-whale
of the Earth Kingdom – Dilberta.

The one whose waist
your arms won't get around – Dilberta.

The mammoth one whose weight
you pray, won't knock you to the ground.

The one who displays toes
like archway windows,
bringing the pads of her feet down
like giant paperweights
to keep the earth from shifting about.

3

Dilberta, rippling as she ambles under
the wrinkled tarpaulin of her skin,
casually throwing the arm of her nose
saying, "Go on, have a stroke".

But sometimes, in her mind's eye,
Dilberta gets this idea – She could be
  a Moth!
Yes, with the wind stirring behind
  her ears,
she could really fly.
Rising above the boundaries of
  the paddock,
Making for the dark light of the forest –
Hearing, O once more, the
  trumpets roar.

Grace Nichols

# Elegy

"Mummy, what was an elephant?"

Each ear was tuned to the forest,
each trunk uncurled to the sun;
each forehead domed against a sky
unchanged since time began.
Each head was raised in greeting
as they swayed from each new dawn,
and the timeless paths of the forest
echoed with trumpet-song.

5

Now the skies are dark,
the paths have gone;
what once was a forest
has turned to stone.
Now only vultures
shadow the sky
and the queens of the forest
are left, to die.

Before we are silenced,
hear our song;
before we are silenced,
hear our cry.

Judith Nicholls

# Elephant

If I could be reincarnated
  (And who knows, I might have been
already?)
Then I'd like to return as an elephant
Reliable and steady.

Big as a room filled with sunshine,
  A giant, gentle and strong,
Lord of the manor
  I'd roam the Savannah
Trumpeting all day long.

At sunset it's down to the river
   To meet my old pals for a chat
After a few bouts of trunk-wrestling
   We'd squirt water, do daft things
   like that.

Then tired and happy we'd lumber home
   Humming an elephant tune
Thinking our thanks to our maker
   By the light of an elephant moon.

11

If I could be reincarnated
   An elephant I would choose,
Failing that, Napoleon,
   Kim Basinger or Ted Hughes.

Roger McGough

12

# Morwenstow

Where do you come from, sea,

To the sharp Cornish shore,

Leaping up to the raven's crag?

**From Labrador.**

Do you grow tired, sea?

Are you weary ever

When the storms burst over your head?

**Never.**

Are you hard as a diamond, sea,
As iron, as oak?
Are you stronger than flint or steel?
  And the lightning stroke.

Ten thousand years and more, sea,
You have gobbled up your fill,
Swallowing stone and slate!
  I am hungry still.

**When will you rest, sea?**

When moon and sun

Ride only fields of salt water

And the land is gone.

Charles Causley

# The River's Story

I remember when life was good.
I shilly-shallied across meadows,
Tumbled down mountains,
I laughed and gurgled through woods,
Stretched and yawned in a myriad
  of floods.
Insects, weightless as sunbeams,
Settled upon my skin to drink.
I wore lily-pads like medals.
Fish, lazy and battle-scarred,
Gossiped beneath them.
The damselflies were my ballerinas,
The pike my ambassadors.
Kingfishers, disguised as rainbows,
Were my secret agents.
It was a sweet time, a gone-time,

A time before factories grew,
Brick by greedy brick,
And left me cowering
In monstrous shadows.

Like drunken giants
They vomited their poisons into me.
Tonight a scattering of vagrant bluebells,
Dwarfed by those same poisons,
Toll my ending.

Children, come and find me if you wish
I am your inheritance.
Behind the derelict housing-estates
You will discover my remnants.
Clogged with garbage and junk
To an open sewer I've shrunk.
I, who have flowed through history,
Who have seen hamlets become villages,
Villages become towns, towns
   become cities,
Am reduced to a trickle of filth
Beneath the still, burning stars.

Brian Patten

# The Newcomer

"There's something new in the river."
The fish said as it swam,
"It's got no scales, no fins, no gills,
And ignores the impassable dam."

"There's something new in the trees,"
I heard a bloated thrush sing,
"It's got no beak, no claws, no feathers,
And not even the ghost of a wing."

23

"There's something new in the warren."
The rabbit said to the doe,
"It's got no fur, no eyes, no paws,
Yet digs deeper than we can go."

"There's something new in the
  whiteness,"
said the snow-bright polar bear,
"I saw its shadow on a glacier
But it left no foot-prints there."

Throughout the animal kingdom
The news was spreading fast –

No beak no claws no feathers
No scales no fur no gills,
It lives in the trees and the water,
In the earth and the snow and the hills,
And it kills and it kills and it kills.

Brian Patten

# The Warm and the Cold

Freezing dusk is closing
  Like a slow trap of steel
On trees and roads and hills and all
  That can no longer feel.
    But the carp is in its depth
      Like a planet in its heaven.
    And the badger in its bedding
      Like a loaf in the oven.
    And the butterfly in its mummy
      Like a viol in a case.
    And the owl in its feathers
      Like a doll in its lace.

Freezing dusk has tightened
  Like a nut screwed tight
On the starry aeroplane
  Of the soaring night.
    But the trout is in its hole
      Like a chuckle in a sleeper.
    The hare strays down the highway
      Like a root going deeper.
    The snail is dry in the outhouse
      Like a seed in a sunflower.
    The owl is pale on the gatepost
      Like a clock on its tower.

Moonlight freezes the shaggy world
  Like a mammoth of ice –
The past and the future
  Are the jaws of a steel vice.
    But the cod is in the tide-rip
      Like a key in a purse.
    The deer are on the bare-blown hill
      Like smiles on a nurse.
    The flies are behind the plaster
      Like the lost score of a jig.
    Sparrows are in the ivy-clump
      Like money in a pig.

Such a frost
  The flimsy moon
    Has lost her wits.

    A star falls.
The sweating farmers
Turn in their sleep
  Like oxen on spits.

Ted Hughes

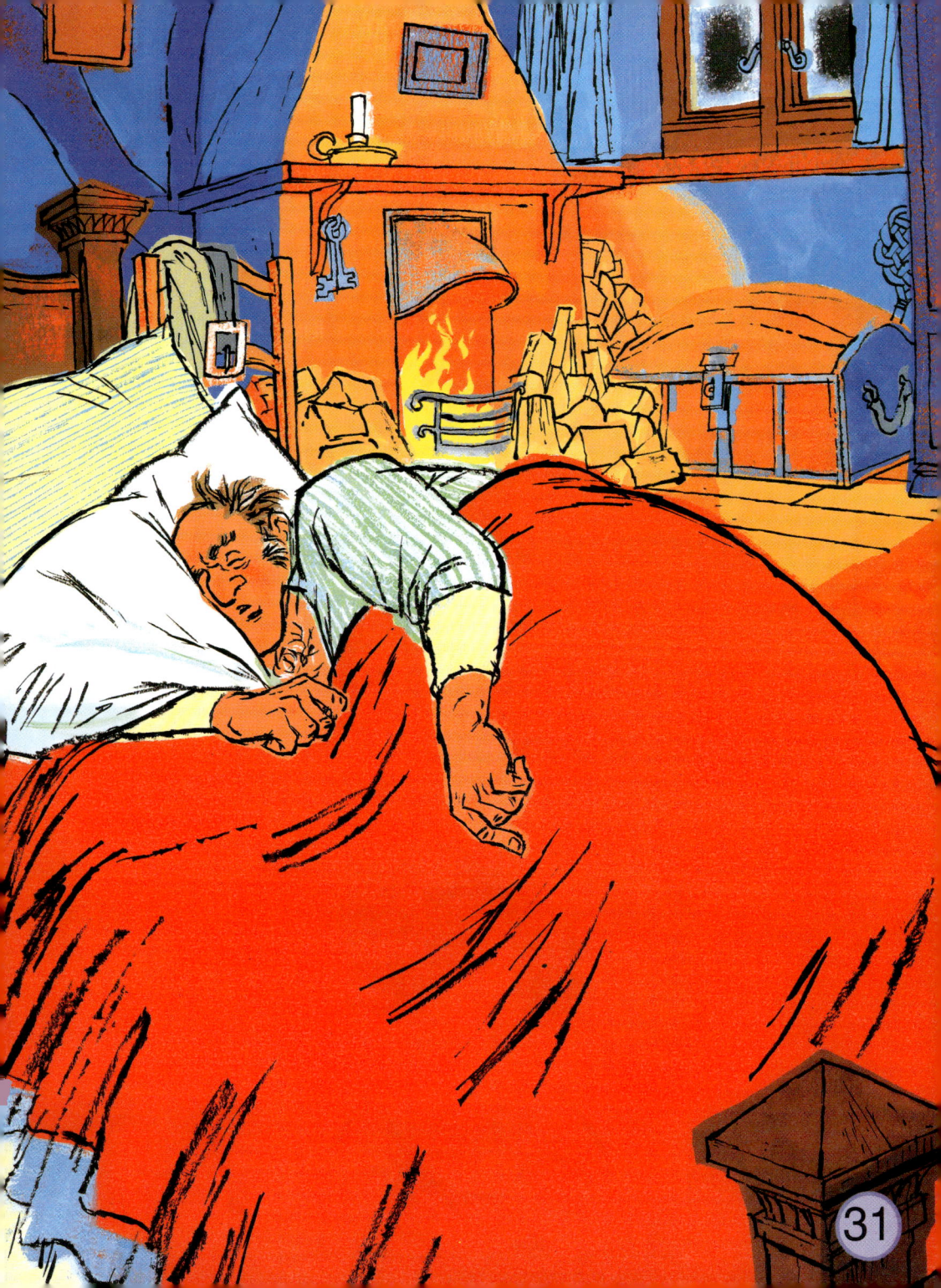

# The Reader of This Poem

The reader of this poem

Is as cracked as a cup

As daft as treacle toffee

As mucky as a pup

As troublesome as bubblegum

As brash as a brush

As bouncy as a double-tum

As quiet as a sshhh...

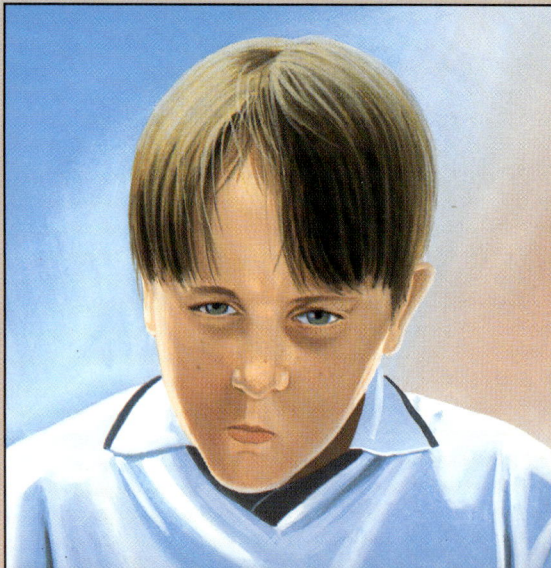

As sneaky as a wizard's spell

As tappy-toe as jazz

As empty as a wishing-well

As echoey as as as as as as... as... as...

As bossy as a whistle

As prickly as a pair

Of boots made out of thistles

And elephant hair

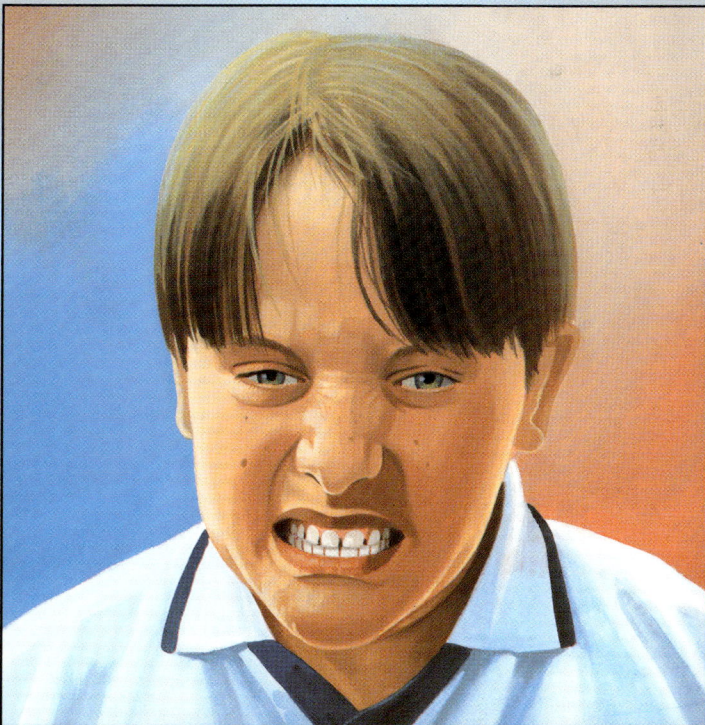

As vain as trainers

As boring as a draw

As smelly as a drain is

Outside a kitchen door


As hungry as a wave

That feeds upon the coast

As gaping as the grave

As GOTCHA! as a ghost

As fruitless as a cake of soap

As creeping-up as smoke

The reader of this poem, I hope,

Knows how to take a joke!

Roger McGough

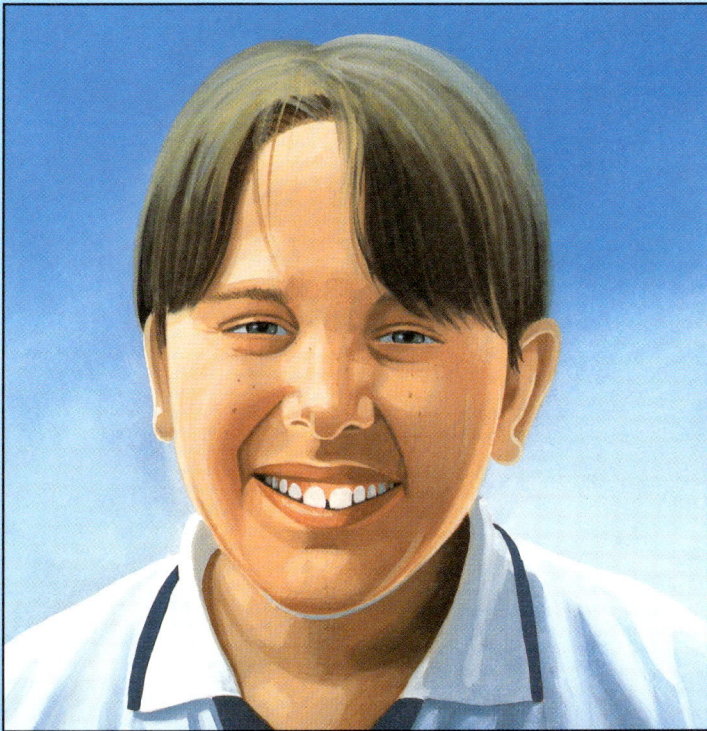

# Crow

A crow is a crow is a crow
In the bird popularity poll
We are the lowest of the low
But do we care? ...

While others twitter on and on, or worse
Bang out the same three notes
Of musical morse, we refrain.
If there's 'owt to caw, we caw.

Long since banned from the dawn chorus

We lie in bed until lunchtime

Then leisurely flap down

And bag a few smug worms.

Potter about in the afternoon
Call on friends, or simply bide.
For the night that others hide from
Is the time that we like best.

Nestled in treetops gently swaying
We stretch out to the sky
And hold court with the moon.
Stargazers we. The thinkers.

Looking deep into the heavens
We drift and drift and drift
Up and up into the blueblack
Into the very crowness of the universe.

A crow is a crow is a crow

In the bird popularity poll

We are the lowest of the low

But do we care? ...

Roger McGough

# Woodpecker

Woodpecker is rubber-necked
   But has a nose of steel.
He bangs his head against the wall
   And cannot even feel.

When woodpecker's jack-hammer head
   Starts up its dreadful din
Knocking the dead bough double dead
   How do his eyes stay in?

Pity the poor dead oak that cries
   In terrors and in pains.
But pity more the woodpecker's eyes
   And bouncing rubber brains.

Ted Hughes

# Forty-One

The door is locked,
the curtains drawn;
the paint has peeled
from years of sun.
But there's no one dare
play "knock and run"
or stand and stare
at forty-one!

For old Mr Dunn
of forty-one
is never seen
till the sun has gone.

There's no letter-box
at forty-one;
no postman knocks
for Mr Dunn.
There's nobody knows
just what goes on
in the silent rooms
of forty-one.

For old Mr Dunn
of forty-one
is never seen
till night has come.

"There's nobody there
at forty-one!"
some may declare;
but I know they're wrong.
For a grey cat prowls
across the lawn
and I've seen a light
where the curtain's torn;
and a shadow creeps
beneath the moon
when midnight strikes
at forty-one.

For old Mr Dunn
of forty-one
steals out of his house
when midnight's come ...

Judith Nicholls

44

# Moon-Gazer

On moonlight night
when moon is bright
Beware, Beware –

Moon-Gazer man
with his throw-back head
and his open legs
gazing, gazing
up at the moon

Moon-Gazer man
with his seal-skin hair
and his round-eye stare
staring, staring
up at the moon

Moon-Gazer man
standing tall,
lamp-post tall,
just gazing up
at moon eye-ball

But never try to pass
between those open legs
cause Moon-Gazer man
will close them with a snap –
you'll be trapped

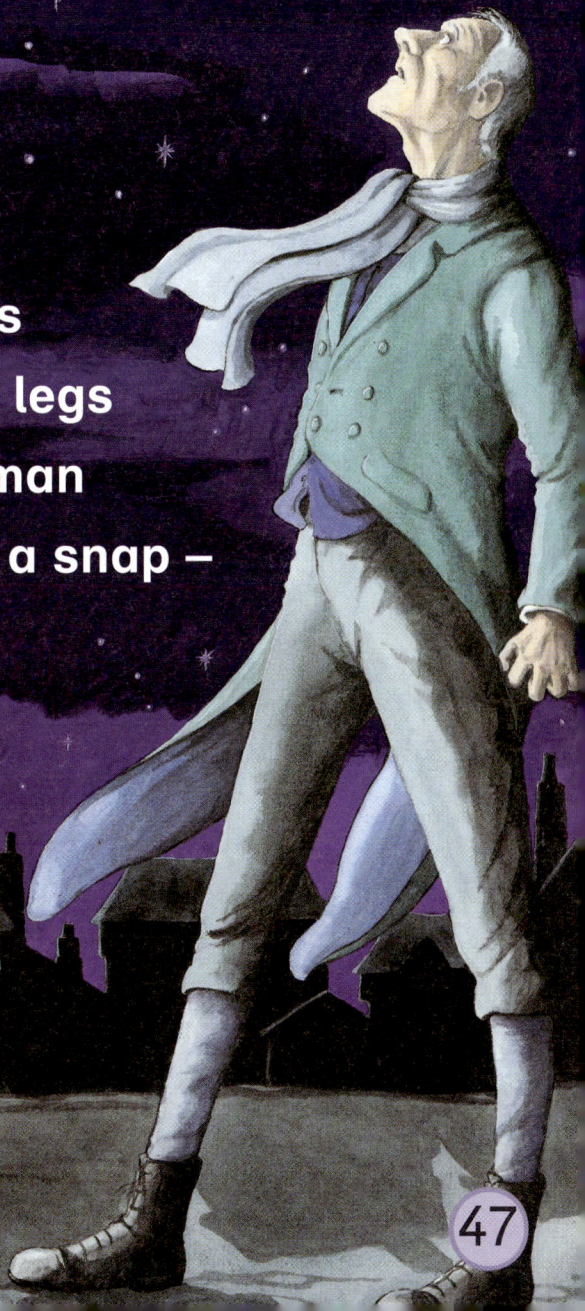

Moon-Gazer man
will crush you flat.
Yes with just one shake
suddenly you'll be –
a human pancake

On moonlight night
when moon is bright
for goodness' sake
stay home –
and pull your window-curtain tight.

Grace Nichols

"Moon-Gazer" is a supernatural folk-figure,
extremely tall, who can be seen mostly straddling
roadways on moonlight nights, gazing up at the
moon. It is best not to pass between his legs.